The Day God Created Grace

DR. TED BEAM

ILLUSTRATED BY ALEX BEAM

ISBN 979-8-88644-436-0 (Paperback)
ISBN 979-8-88644-437-7 (Digital)

Covenant Books
11661 Hwy 707
Murrells Inlet, SC 29576
www.covenantbooks.com

To my wife, Debbie, and to our children, Ariel, Alexander, Alissa, and Amelia.

CONTENTS

PREFACE

During the summer when I was eleven years old, I stood in our backyard remembering the football game we had played the day before. My dad was home for the summer. As a teacher and as a coach, he was busy during the school year, but in the summer we got to spend time with him.

A bunch of my friends had come over to our backyard for a football game. Dad was the all-time quarterback for both teams. Instead of mowing the grass, we played football. It was a great day.

I stood there in the yard remembering that game the day before. I remembered the passes I had caught from Dad. I remembered the runs made by my friends. I remembered the pile-up tackles. And I also remembered the laughter. We had so much fun. As I stood there, I found myself praying for my own children for the first time, "God, if you give me a son, I will raise him the same way my dad is raising me."

God gave me that son almost thirty years later. During those thirty years, I began praying also for my daughters whom God might give to me. As a boy, I knew mostly about boys. But as a future father, I figured out that I might have some daughters also. So I started praying for them as well.

My first daughter, Ariel, taught me that I could love someone with my whole heart in just an instant as I held her for the first time. I learned the same thing with each of my four children. Ariel and I danced around the hospital room as I sang to her. While growing up, she won many state titles in power tumbling and trampoline as well as several national titles on trampoline. I remember her at ten years of age standing on the pedals of her bicycle, zooming down the street, her arms stretched out to the sides and the wind blowing through her hair.

My son Alexander grew up participating in Cub Scouts and Boy Scouts. He earned his Eagle Scout rank less than two weeks before his eighteenth birthday. He enjoys people, and he makes friends everywhere he goes. In school, he played football, basketball, wrestling, and track and field. He has learned that some goals take years to accomplish.

My daughter Alissa sings well. We enjoy listening to her sing at school talent shows and church events. She doesn't know that we also enjoy listening to her sing around the house. She studies well and participates in the girls' wrestling team at her school. The team has won back-to-back state championships. Alissa is courageous and works hard. She enjoys reading stories about the Greek gods and about great adventures.

My youngest daughter, Amelia, is involved in Girl Scouts. She is kind-hearted and compassionate. She seeks out her friends who are hurting, and she listens to them for as long as they need to talk. She enjoys assembling 3-D puzzles and watching YouTube videos of various family games and activities. She also enjoys baking cookies as well as designing and conducting scavenger hunts.

All four of my children have grown into courageous people. They have learned to take responsibility for each of their decisions. They are honest and compassionate, and they enjoy the life Jesus has given to each of them.

When I was growing up, our sixth-grade class voted my wife, Debbie, as the most intelligent girl in the sixth grade. After that, I started watching her from across the room. When I realized how smart she was, she became more attractive to me. Even though she has very pretty eyes and her eyes sparkle whenever she smiles and she is breathtakingly beautiful, her intelligence was and still is the most attractive feature for me. Her mind is amazing.

It took me six more years before I built up enough courage to ask Debbie for a date. We went to a movie called *Raiders of the Lost Ark* and then we went to McDonald's. She ate two bites of a cheeseburger while I ate two Big Macs and the rest of her cheeseburger.

We went on that date on Friday the 13th of November. So we have treated Friday the 13th as good luck for us.

Debbie and I have worked hard to teach each of our children to read. We appreciate the public schools and the teachers, but we did not rely on them to teach our children to read. We knew that if our children learned to read well, then they could use reading to learn anything they wanted to learn throughout their entire lives.

In addition to doing a great job rearing our four children, Debbie has been involved in children's ministries at our churches for over thirty years. After twenty years as a volunteer, our church hired Debbie as the children's pastor. We have enjoyed working together in helping children learn about Jesus Christ, the Savior of the world. Whether she is a paid children's pastor or a volunteer, she is the best children's pastor I have known.

During her many years in ministry to children in our churches, she has also helped at summer camps in their children's ministries. She has helped to guide over two hundred children to give their hearts to Jesus during Vacation Bible School, during Sunday school classes and Christmas plays, at summer camps, and in a variety of other activities.

So when I decided to write this book for children about the garden of Eden, I wanted you to know about Debbie. I wanted you to know that she has helped many children come to know Jesus as their Savior. I also wanted you to know a little bit about our children. We wanted each one of our children. We asked Jesus to give us each one of our children.

I have shared with them about the garden of Eden. Through this book, I want to share this wonderful information with you as well.

I hope you enjoy reading this book. I have prayed for you that God will help you to understand his love and will help you to receive his love. I have titled this book *The Day God Created Grace*. I have prayed for you as well that God will help you to open your heart to receive his grace.

ACKNOWLEDGMENTS

Many thanks to Benjamin Kerchner for his patience and wise guidance with me on this book. I also want to thank Sheree Pruett, acquisitions agent for giving me, an unknown this opportunity, and for giving my young illustrator this opportunity. And many thanks to the entire team at Covenant Books.

CHAPTER 1

God Created Our Potential

What is your favorite fruit? Did you know that over twenty different kinds of bananas grow throughout the tropical regions of the world? Have you learned about Johnny Appleseed who walked across North America while he scattered apple seeds that later sprouted and grew into apple trees?

Do you like kiwi? Lemons? Avocados? Mangoes? Have you seen coconuts growing on a palm tree near the ocean? Have you ever tasted a kumquat, a star fruit, or a persimmon? How many different kinds of fruit have you eaten just this week?

In Genesis, the first book of the Bible, in the second chapter, God tells Adam that he has planted thousands of fruit trees: "Out of the ground the LORD God caused to grow every tree that is pleasing to the sight and good for food" (Genesis 2:9). God tells Adam that he may eat from them all: "The LORD God commanded the man, saying, 'From any tree of the garden you may eat freely'" (Genesis 2:16).

Can you imagine thousands of fruit trees? Can you imagine entire orchards of plums, pears, peaches, pineapples, papayas, and pomegranates growing across the meadows throughout the garden of Eden? Try to imagine entire groves of navel oranges and fig trees reaching branch to branch around the perimeter of the garden. Do you think God built special grape arbors for the grapevines, or do you think they might have wrapped around the tree trunks as they climbed high into the leaf canopy?

Do you notice that a pear is bigger at the bottom and smaller at the stem while an apple is bigger at the stem and smaller at the bottom? Pretend for a moment that you reach up and pick a Granny

Smith apple from a tree. While other apples are red or yellow, do you notice the shiny green skin of that Granny Smith apple?

Instead of biting into the apple, take a knife and cut the apple in half. Do not cut it down from the stem through the core. Instead, cut it across the middle so you can see a cross section of the core. Do you see the shape of the core?

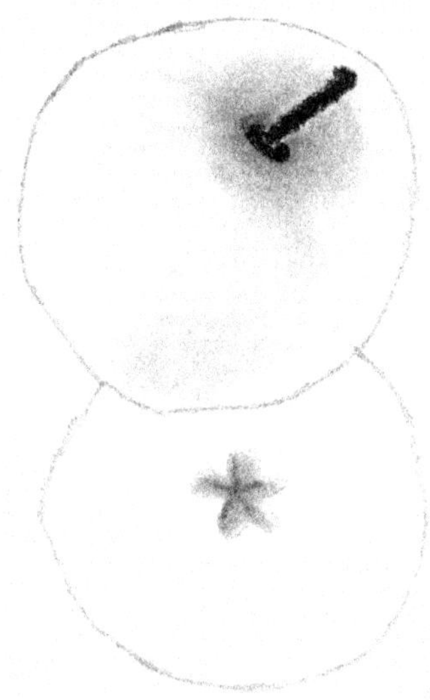

Can you see the five-pointed star outline made by the seed pockets in the core of that apple? Does it remind you of the billions of stars God splashed across the universe that all shine in the night sky?

As you look at that apple, how many seeds do you count? Most apples will have anywhere from three to ten seeds in the core pockets. You can count them. But have you ever wondered how many apples can grow from each seed once each seed is planted?

God designed the apple that way. He wants it to have great potential just like he created you to have great potential. Even though the world has only one of you, God wants you to reproduce your kindness to other people. God wants you to reproduce your perseverance or your patience in other people. God wants you to reproduce your friendship with other people.

Have you ever noticed that we have green apples, red apples, yellow apples, and even some apples with mixed colors? Each one has shiny skin. Each one provides nutrition which can help us to stay healthy. Each apple looks pretty much the same on the inside with the star-shaped core pockets full of seeds. Each seed has great potential for millions of new apples.

Just like apples have different skin colors, people have different skin colors. Just like apples are the same on the inside, many people are the same on the inside also. Maybe God wants us to use the apples he created to learn how to see value in other people who have a different skin color than we do. Maybe God wants you to make friends with boys or girls who have different skin colors than you do.

In that same chapter of the Bible, Genesis records for us that God created a huge river that flowed through the garden of Eden: "Now a river flowed out of Eden to water the garden; and from there it divided" (Genesis 2:10). As the river flowed through the garden, it divided into four smaller rivers named the Pishon, the Gihon, the Tigris, and the Euphrates (Genesis 2:10–14). We do not have a lot of information about the Pishon and the Gihon, but we can see the Tigris River and the Euphrates River as they flow today through the countries of Turkey, Syria, and Iraq. By looking at a map, you can trace these rivers as they flow into the Persian Gulf.

When astronauts began to fly in space we learned how big the Tigris River and the Euphrates River really are. They are so big that astronauts can see them from space. This helps us to discover that the garden of Eden was a very big place.

Instead of the garden of Eden being the size of a garden with green beans and tomatoes like the one in your city park or backyard, the garden of Eden was probably closer to the size of the Amazon Jungle in South America. When you look on a map, you can see that the Amazon Jungle is about half the size of the United States.

While you imagine the trees and the rivers, can you also imagine feeling the breeze as it ruffles your hair? Can you imagine smelling the pink or purple blossoms of all those fruit trees? I wonder if the sweet aroma of honeysuckle floated on the breeze as it blew across the meadow. Can you imagine smelling the pink, blue, purple, orange, or red orchids as they sprouted up within the meadow? What might you have smelled in that beautiful garden?

Adam and Eve lived in the garden of Eden. The Bible does not tell us how long they lived there. The Bible does record for us that God created it as a very beautiful place to live. The Bible also tells us that God placed two very special trees in the center of the garden. Let's take a longer look at those two trees.

CHAPTER 2

God Created Our Five Senses

God placed two special trees in the middle of the garden of Eden: "the tree of life also in the midst of the garden, and the tree of the knowledge of good and evil" (Genesis 2:9). The Bible does not tell us much about the tree of life. The Bible does not describe the fruit. We do not know its size, its shape, or its color. The Bible records for us that it grew in the middle of the garden along with the tree of the knowledge of good and evil.

The Bible records for us that the tree of life still exists but now grows in heaven: "On either side of the river was the tree of life, bearing twelve kinds of fruit, yielding its fruit every month; and the leaves of the tree were for the healing of the nations" (Revelation 22:2). The Bible describes the tree of life in heaven as having twelve different kinds of fruit ripening every month and the leaves bring healing to people.

The Bible tells us some things about the other special tree, the tree of the knowledge of good and evil. Just like the tree of life, the Bible does not tell us what kind of fruit grew on this tree. Often people talk about the *apple*, but the Bible really does not tell us. We do not know the shape, texture, size, or color of its fruit.

We do know that God told Adam and Eve to leave it alone. We do know that God told them not to eat from this tree. We do know that it grew in the middle of the garden. And we do know that God told Adam, "The day that you eat from it you will surely die" (Genesis 2:17).

Why do you think this tree grew in the middle of the garden? God told Adam that if he ate from the tree, he would die that same day. Would you want something dangerous right in the middle of the room where everyone could reach it? Why not have it grow way out on the edge somewhere, maybe even hidden behind a thousand other trees?

We do not know God's reason for placing it in the middle of the garden, but I suspect it might have to do with trusting God and with obeying God. So it would make sense to put that tree right in the center of life for Adam and Eve. In other words, trusting God and obeying God together make up the central, most important things in our lives.

The Bible tells us that if Adam and Eve obeyed God and left the tree alone, they would live. If they did not obey God and they ate from the tree of the knowledge of good and evil, they would gain some special knowledge. They would know good and evil. And they would die (Genesis 2:17).

Even with the good and the evil, did you know that God created at least two kinds of knowledge? One kind is the knowledge you gain by watching and listening from a distance. We call that observational knowledge. We can gain this knowledge by using our five senses to see, hear, taste, touch, and smell. We observe other people doing things, or we observe other activities.

We watch a friend throw a ball up into the air, and then the ball comes back down. Then she does it again. After watching her throw the ball five or six times, we learn that if we throw a ball into the air, it will come back down. We learn this by observing the action. What else have you learned by observing activities around you?

What have you learned by observing other things? Have you noticed that the buzzard's wings point up toward the sky and the hawk's wings stretch out parallel with the ground? Have you noticed that a hummingbird flies backward as it hovers near a flower? Have you watched the woodpecker flap its wings five or six times and then fold its wings against its body and soar through the air like an arrow?

Have you ever watched a squirrel climb? Have you learned that other people have different colored hair, and some of them change the color of their hair? Have you learned that other people grow to different heights? Some are short. Some are tall. Some have blue eyes or green eyes, while others have brown eyes.

Some people live in the United States and some people live in the Fiji Islands or they live in Egypt or they live in another nation altogether. Did you know that we have over two hundred nations in the world? Using our five senses to observe is the kind of learning you do whenever you read a book or a street sign, or the label on a box of cereal, or maybe the signs at the zoo where each animal is displayed telling us about that animal. All these are examples of observational knowledge.

We call the other kind of knowledge experiential knowledge. We gain this knowledge also through our five senses by experiencing something directly for ourselves. We learn from our own experience what a flower smells like or what a pig smells like. Have you noticed how sugar tastes different than salt? By touching a pine tree we can learn some ways its sap differs from the sap of a maple tree.

We hear the sound of thunder or the sound of the birds singing in the morning. Maybe you have felt your hair pulled back by the wind as you have run down the street or across the field. Or maybe you have learned how it feels to have raindrops land on your face. Maybe you have seen how the sun shines brightly in the middle of the sky and how it seems to lessen its brightness during a colorful sunset.

Our five senses help us also to experience our emotions. If we cannot reach the top shelf in the grocery store, we know from our own experience what it feels like to be short. This might cause us to feel frustrated or cause us to wish we were taller. If we go to sleep at night without eating something, we might know from our own experience what it feels like to be hungry. This can cause us to feel fear wondering if we will have food tomorrow.

Maybe you have learned that ice cream tastes cold and has many wonderful flavors. Eating ice cream can cause us to feel happy. These things and many others we learn from our own experience.

CHAPTER 3
God Created Satan

The Bible teaches us that the devil or Satan came to Eve in the garden of Eden and tried to get her to disobey God (Genesis 3:1–7). The Bible tells us that the serpent spoke to Eve.

Have you ever had someone tease you? Have you had someone tease you so much that you got angry? When that happened, you might have called him a mean name, trying to get back at him.

Sometimes people call that kind of person a skunk or a jerk. Sometimes they call that person a *dirty rotten snake.* Satan was that kind of a dirty, rotten snake in the garden of Eden. He still is today. He tries to get us to disobey God just like he tried to get Eve to disobey God.

Before we take a look at how Satan convinced Eve to eat the forbidden fruit, let's take a good look at him. When the Bible introduces him in Genesis, the Bible records for us that God made him: "Now the serpent was more crafty than any beast of the field the LORD God had made" (Genesis 3:1). He is not an evil god. He is not a competitor with God.

Other religions around the world have good gods and evil gods. Sometimes the good gods win the battle, and sometimes the evil gods win the battle. God and Satan did not exist together as enemies in heaven. The Bible is clear that God made Satan. Now, let's take a closer look at how God made him.

Satan was named Lucifer originally. The prophet Ezekiel records for us that Satan started out as the anointed cherub: "You were the anointed cherub who covers" (Ezekiel 28:14). God made him an archangel along with Michael the archangel and Gabriel the archangel.

God made Michael the archangel to be the leader of all the angel armies of heaven.

> And there was war in heaven, Michael and his angels waging war with the dragon. The dragon and his angels waged war, and they were not strong enough, and there was no longer a place found for them in heaven. And the great dragon was thrown down, the serpent of old who is called the devil and Satan. (Revelation 12:7–9)

God made Gabriel the archangel to be his number-one messenger. Gabriel took a message from God to Daniel explaining visions about the future (Daniel 9:20–23, 10:12–14). Gabriel told Zacharias he would be the father of John the Baptist (Luke 1:8–20). Gabriel told Mary she would give birth to Jesus (Luke 1:26–38).

The prophet Ezekiel describes Satan as being in Eden, the garden of God (Ezekiel 28:11–19, Genesis 3:1–7). That gave Satan special access to Adam and Eve. He could talk with them. He could walk with them.

Many people want to know why God allowed Satan to tempt Eve like he did. Many people wish God had kept Satan away from

Eve. So let me ask you one question. Which do you enjoy more, a hug from your toy stuffed animal or a hug from your best friend?

Most of us know a hug really doesn't count if we did not choose to hug. God knew it did not count for Eve to trust him and obey him unless she chose to do so. If God made her do it, it would not count.

God made it possible for Eve to reject him. If she could not push him away, then when she hugged him, it would not count. So God gave Eve the ability to choose what she would do. By creating her with that ability, when she chose to love God, it would count.

God gave Eve the ability to choose, to have a free will. Satan took advantage of that free will to tempt Eve. Eve had the equal choice to trust God and to obey God or not to trust God and not to obey God.

God has given you that same power and authority we call a free will. You make the decision to obey or disobey your parents or to obey or disobey your teacher. You make the decision to respect your grandmother or to disrespect your grandmother. You make the decision to eat healthy food or to push away healthy food. You make the decision to watch things secretly on the computer that you are not supposed to watch or not to watch them. You make the decision to smoke and Vape or not to smoke and Vape. You make the decision to drink alcohol or not to drink alcohol. God gave you the power and the authority to have your own free will.

When God created Satan, God created him with extra beauty and wisdom: "You had the seal of perfection, full of wisdom and perfect in beauty" (Ezekiel 28:12). Satan shined brighter than all the other angels. God decorated him with many precious stones found in different colors like the deep-yellow topaz or sky-blue topaz or the rainforest-green topaz.

> Every precious stone was your covering: the ruby, the topaz and the diamond; the beryl, the onyx and the jasper; the lapis lazuli, the turquoise and the emerald; and the gold, the workmanship of your settings and sockets, was in you on the day that you were created. (Ezekiel 28:13)

God adorned him with the beryl, which you can find in pink, blue, green, yellow, and red. God embellished him with the black onyx, the red jasper stone, and the blue jasper stone. God decorated him with the green and blue precious stones of turquoise, emerald, and lapis lazuli. God placed all of these jewels in gold settings.

God accessorized Satan with gold and jewels, causing him to glow and sparkle with beauty. The apostle Paul alludes to this beauty when he describes Satan as an angel of light: "Even Satan disguises himself as an angel of light" (2 Corinthians 11:14). God used his wonderful creativity to decorate Satan with many colored precious jewels. God even included the ruby and the diamond.

In addition to Satan's physical beauty, Ezekiel continues his description of Satan by writing that God created him as blameless before God: "You were blameless in your ways from the day you were created" (Ezekiel 28:15). Satan worshiped and served God with all his heart.

Satan led all the angels in singing as they worshiped God. Satan blended the choirs of heaven. Like rolling thunder, the basses and baritones rumbled through the sky. He brought in the altos and featured the sopranos who split the stars with their highest of notes. Satan led the choir in singing to the glory of God, but only for a while.

We do not know how long, but after a while, violence and destruction emerged in Satan's heart.

> You were blameless in your ways from the day you were created until unrighteousness was found in you. By the abundance of your trade you were internally filled with violence, and you sinned; therefore I have cast you as profane from the mountain of God. And I have destroyed you, O covering cherub, from the midst of the stones of fire. Your heart was lifted up because of your beauty; you corrupted your wisdom by reason of your splendor. I cast you to the ground. (Ezekiel 28:15–17)

Ezekiel explains that Satan began to enjoy looking at his own beauty more than he enjoyed looking at God. He admired the shine of his gold. He danced to the sparkle of his jewels. Within his own heart, Satan began to consider himself as beautiful as God and as important as God. Isaiah records for us that Satan desired to sit on the throne of heaven.

> But you said in your heart, "I will ascend to heaven; I will raise my throne above the stars of God, and I will sit on the mount of assembly in the recesses of the north. I will ascend above the heights of the clouds; I will make myself like the Most High." (Isaiah 14:13–14)

Satan began to rage inside himself because God treated him like a creature instead of like a co-creator. Satan's hatred for God overshadowed any love for God he had felt previously.

These changes in Satan's heart disappointed God and caused great sadness in God's heart. God wondered about how to help Satan return to honesty, but Satan grew more angry and more defiant each day. God ordered Michael the archangel, the general of all the armies of heaven, to go to battle against Satan and to throw him out of heaven.

> And there was war in heaven, Michael and his angels waging war with the dragon. The dragon and his angels waged war, and they were not strong enough, and there was no longer a place found for them in heaven. And the great dragon was thrown down, the serpent of old who is called the devil and Satan, who deceives the whole world; he was thrown down to the earth, and his angels were thrown down with him. (Revelation 12:7–9)

The battle lasted a long time. Some angels rode on great white stallions while others flew. Angels used bows and arrows. They used swords and shields. During this battle we discovered that Satan had recruited one-third of all the angels to join him in rebelling against God: "And his tail swept away a third of the stars of heaven and threw them to the earth" (Revelation 12:4). He had thousands and thousands of angels take up their swords and fight against Michael and his armies.

> And there was war in heaven, Michael and his angels waging war with the dragon. The dragon and his angels waged war; and they were not strong enough, and there was no longer a place found for them in heaven. And the great dragon was thrown down, the serpent of old who is called the devil and Satan, who deceives the whole world; he was thrown down to the earth, and his angels were thrown down with him. Then I heard a loud voice in heaven, saying, "Now the salvation, and the power, and the kingdom of our God and the authority of His Christ have come, for the accuser of our brethren has been thrown down, he who accuses them before our God day and night. And they overcame him because of the blood of the Lamb and because of the word of their testimony, and they did not love their life even when faced with death. For this reason, rejoice, O heavens and you who dwell in them. Woe to the earth and the sea, because the devil has come down to you, having great wrath, knowing that he has only a short time."
> (Revelation 12:7–12)

The book of Revelation teaches us that Satan and the angels he recruited became demons and are called stars as a secret code word (Revelation 12:4). This helps us to understand the secret code the prophet Isaiah used when he called Satan the "star of the morning" (Isaiah 14:12). In Revelation, we are told that one-third of the stars are thrown out of heaven with the dragon, another code word for Satan. He swung his tail and took one-third of the angels with him (Revelation 12:4).

We learn from Isaiah that Satan wanted to climb to the top of heaven and sit on the throne of God (Isaiah 14:12–15). Satan wanted to shove God off the throne and climb onto the throne himself. He wanted to rule heaven and earth. He wanted all the angels of heaven to worship him instead of worshiping God.

Satan's jealousy of God showed up in violence and destruction. Satan wanted to conquer God, but he could not. Remember, God created him. Satan is not an evil god. He is not equal to God. So as a creature, Satan can never really challenge God, because God is the one and only Creator.

Satan cannot challenge God, but he can challenge the other archangels. The Bible records for us that God created three archangels. Satan was full of beauty and led all the angels to worship God. God created Michael to lead the armies of heaven. God created Gabriel to be the chief messenger. Here is an example of Satan's battles with the other two archangels.

When God sent Gabriel to give a message to Daniel, Satan blocked Gabriel's way (Daniel 9–10). Daniel calls Satan the Prince of Persia (Daniel 10:13). Daniel writes about Michael, who came to escort Gabriel past Satan so Gabriel could deliver the message to Daniel.

> But the prince of the kingdom of Persia
> was withstanding me for twenty-one days; then
> behold, Michael, one of the chief princes, came
> to help me, for I had been left there with the
> kings of Persia. (Daniel 10:13)

This passage of the Bible, Daniel 9–10, tells about all three archangels. Even in this one verse I have quoted for you, can you identify the secret code words used to speak about the archangels and the other angels? After you take a moment to identify the secret code words, let's go back to the garden of Eden.

God allowed Satan to enter the garden of Eden. Satan hates God a lot. Since Satan could not beat God and sit on the throne of heaven, he could think of only one other way to hurt God. Satan knew he would hurt God even more by harming the very people God loved. So Satan decided to convince Adam and Eve to reject God.

Satan still does this today. God loves you with all his heart. Satan knows that if he can get you to distrust God, that will hurt God. If Satan can convince you that God is a problem, then you will not give your heart to God. If Satan can get you to suspect God is holding you back somehow, then Satan can hurt God by keeping you and God apart from each other.

Now let's look at how Satan did this with Eve (Genesis 3:1–7). He started by trying to confuse Eve about God's motives. Satan wanted Eve to suspect God and stop trusting God. Satan asked Eve, "Did God say, 'you shall not eat from any tree of the garden?'" (Genesis 3:1). He tried to confuse her.

Satan does the same thing today when he has your friend ask, "Do you obey your mom all the time?" He has your friend use the word *all* to try to confuse you. He wants you to disobey your mom. He wants to cause trouble between you and your mom. This will cause trouble between you and God also. So Satan uses your friend's question to get you to disobey your mom this one time. This is how Satan got Eve to turn her attention to the one thing that God had said not to do.

Remember God gave Adam and Eve thousands of fruit trees. They could eat from them all. God just wanted them to avoid eating from the one tree. So, by asking questions and accusing God of holding back something wonderful, Satan got Eve to focus her attention on the one tree God told her to avoid. Satan changed some words that changed the meanings. Satan told only part of the story. Satan exaggerated. Satan said things like "Did God really say you are not allowed to eat from this tree?"

Satan wanted Eve to forget the many, many other trees and just focus on what she should not have. He does the same thing today. Instead of enjoying the toys we have and the friends we have, Satan gets us to look at what other people have. He convinces us we would be happier if we had other toys or other friends. He gets us distracted and tries to convince us we are unhappy. He gets us to focus on what we do not have.

While Eve began to think about the one tree, she began to feel unhappy. She grew suspicious of God and began to wonder, *Why would God hold back that special knowledge? Why would God want me not to experience everything wonderful?* At that very moment, Satan said another thing, "You surely will not die. For God knows that in the day you eat from it your eyes will be opened, and you will be like God knowing good and evil" (Genesis 3:4–5).

Satan wanted Eve to become jealous of God. He wanted Eve to stop trusting God. He wanted Eve to turn away from God who loved her and who gave her life. Satan wanted Eve to harm herself and die.

Eve began to figure out a way to eat the fruit. She looked at it for a long time and said to herself, *The fruit is very pretty. It would look good in my hand. It's nutritious. And it promises to give special knowledge.* So the Bible records for us that she thought of those reasons why she should eat the fruit.

Eve wanted to eat the forbidden fruit. So Eve began to figure out a way to talk herself into eating the fruit. Eve thought about the fruit's appearance. It was pretty. She might have thought about how the fruit would give her special nutrition, *After all, God wants me to be healthy, right?* And then she thought that if she ate the fruit, it would make her wise like God.

Eve reached her hand toward the closest piece of fruit on the tree. Then she pulled her hand back. She had never experienced this sort of struggle within herself before. She wanted to eat the fruit, but she also wanted to avoid it. She wanted to trust God, but she had grown suspicious that God was holding her back.

She decided to take just one piece, a small piece. She looked at it. She held it. She turned it over and over in her hands. It felt smooth and pleasant. It did not feel dangerous at all. Maybe God had exaggerated. Maybe she could eat it, and maybe she would not die. She certainly had no trouble holding it.

Opening her mouth and sticking out her tongue, she licked the fruit, just one lick and waited. Nothing happened. Not one bad thing happened, so she sunk her teeth deep into the fruit and again waited. She hesitated to pull off that first bite. The juice rolled down her chin. Delicious. Amazing.

Eve had never tasted anything even a little bit like it in all her life. Her eyes closed as she broke off that first bite and savored every chew. Juice popped and fizzled in her mouth. She wiped the juice off her chin and licked it from her hand. She just had to have Adam taste this wonderful treat.

Adam stood behind her among the black raspberries. By looking at her face, seeing the gleam in her eyes and the sunlight glistening off the juice streaks down to her chin, he had watched Eve take a bite from the forbidden fruit. Adam understood at once what had happened. Eve smiled and handed him the fruit. "It's okay," she whispered. "Nothing happened. It's incredible."

Adam knew God had said that if he ate that fruit, he would die. Eve stood there beaming, sunlight glistening through her hair. She was not dead. Adam could see the fruit where Eve had taken a bite.

The fruit had not harmed her at all it seemed. He wondered, *Did God lie to us?*

So Adam took the fruit from Eve's hand. He studied every part of her face. He looked at her nose. It was not twitching. He looked at her mouth. It was not drawn up as if she had swallowed something sour or bitter. He looked into her eyes. He had never seen such excitement and adventure in her eyes before that moment. Adam thought, *Maybe God had lied. Maybe God was the problem.*

Then slowly lifting the fruit, Adam looked at it more closely. The aroma drifted up to him. It smelled kind of sweet and salty all at the same time. He took a bite from the fruit. It tasted even better than it had smelled. The juice ran down his chin also. He also closed his eyes savoring every chew. Then he swallowed, and when he swallowed, both he and Eve began to experience something new, brand new.

CHAPTER 4

Sin Has Symptoms

At first, Adam and Eve felt just a tickle, maybe a tingle in their belly, but in less time than it takes you to take seven long breaths, that tickle and tingle turned into a slight feeling of nausea. They had not felt sick before. This slight nausea came as a brand-new feeling, a brand-new experience. They did not know previously about sickness and disease.

One day, much earlier while Adam chased Eve around the papaya trees, they experienced some dizziness, but that feeling resulted from their playfulness. They enjoyed it. This dizziness, along with the nausea, did not come from their play. It was not enjoyable. Something was wrong, dead wrong. What was this strange new sensation?

They glanced at each other wondering if they each felt the same thing. While they glanced at each other, it happened. Shame and fear avalanched through their souls. Adam saw that Eve was naked. Eve saw that Adam was naked. Well, they had always been naked, but this was different. For the first time they each knew the other one was looking at them.

They each feared that the other one would point and laugh. They grabbed the big leaves from the fig trees and tried to cover their bodies quickly.

> Then the eyes of both of them were opened,
> and they knew that they were naked; and they
> sewed fig leaves together and made themselves
> loin coverings. (Genesis 3:7)

They wanted to hide from each other. They even wanted to hide from themselves if you can do that sort of thing. Mostly they wanted to hide from God.

Adam and Eve had gone past observing and learning. They now experienced everything God had hoped they would avoid. As a result of not trusting God, as a result of disobeying God, they now experienced all the symptoms of guilt, shame, and fear for the very first time.

They no longer felt secure in each other's unconditional acceptance and unconditional love. Adam feared Eve loved him conditionally and might reject him. Eve feared Adam loved her conditionally and might reject her. So let's try to understand what happened when Adam and Eve invited sin into their lives, swallowing it, juice and all.

When you are sick and you go to the doctor or to the clinic, the nurse asks you, "What's wrong today?" When you answer, you start to say things like "I have a runny nose" or "I am coughing" or "I have pain" or "My throat hurts" or "My stomach hurts" or "My eyes are watering" or "I have a headache." All of these things are symptoms. None of these things are the problem.

The nurse swabs your throat, takes your temperature, counts your breaths, checks your pulse, and measures your blood pressure. The doctor listens to your heart and to your lungs. She looks in your ears and eyes and throat. The doctor does all these things to try to identify all the symptoms. Once she identifies all the symptoms, then she can figure out the cause of your illness.

When the doctor discerns what is causing your symptoms, she then gives you medicine that will kill the germs and stop the symptoms. She does all these things hoping to make you feel better. The symptoms help to identify the cause. The symptoms are not the problem. The problem causes the symptoms. The doctor wants to treat the cause.

Adam and Eve did not experience sin. They experienced the symptoms of sin. Sin was the cause of Adam and Eve's shame and fear.

Adam and Eve began feeling new sensations, brand-new emotions. They began to experience guilt, shame, and fear in many forms.

For the very first time in their lives, for the very first time ever for anyone, Adam and Eve felt guilty. They felt ashamed for what they had done. And they felt ashamed of themselves. Because they also heard God walking and calling for them, they feared God: "I heard the sound of You in the garden, and I was afraid because I was naked; so I hid myself" (Genesis 3:10). They feared God would be disappointed in them. They feared he would punish them.

The Bible explains that these three emotions—guilt, shame, and fear—are the symptoms of sin. The Bible identifies sin as the root cause. Sin is the problem. We do not experience sin just like we do not experience a virus. We experience a sore throat, a runny nose, a cough, and fatigue all caused by a virus just like we experience the symptoms of guilt, shame, and fear all caused by sin.

Every day God would come to the garden to visit. Some days they played games together. Some days they sat and visited. Some days they took walks among the trees or waded in the rivers. So when God came that specific day, calling for Adam, both Adam and Eve felt fear and hid themselves from God.

> They heard the sound of the LORD God
> walking in the garden in the cool of the day, and

the man and his wife hid themselves from the
presence of the LORD God among the trees of the
garden. (Genesis 3:8)

They feared God would discover they had eaten from the tree
of the knowledge of good and evil. They feared God would notice a
piece of fruit had been picked off the tree. They feared God would
smell the scent of the juice that had fallen to the ground. They feared
God (Genesis 3:10).

Now I want you to think about this for a moment. Does it
make sense to fear God who loves you unconditionally? Does it make
sense for Adam and Eve to fear God who has given them thousands
of fruit trees? God had knelt on the ground and was the first person
to get dirt under his fingernails as he created Adam from the dirt
of the ground: "Then the LORD God formed man of dust from the
ground" (Genesis 2:7).

Then God leaned over and breathed into Adam similar to the
way many people have learned to perform mouth-to-mouth resusci-
tation, only with Adam, God breathed into his nostrils (Genesis 2:7).
With that breath from God, Adam became alive. Does it make sense
to fear the God who created you and gave you life?

Later, God told Adam that it was not good for him to be alone
(Genesis 2:18). After God made the animals, he brought them to
Adam to have Adam name them (Genesis 2:19). After Adam named
the animals, and after God saw that none of the animals would serve
as a good mate for Adam, God made Adam fall fast asleep.

While Adam slept, God took a rib from Adam, and from that
rib, God built Eve.

So the LORD God caused a deep sleep to fall
upon the man, and he slept; then He took one of
his ribs and closed up the flesh at that place. The
LORD God fashioned into a woman the rib which
He had taken from the man, and brought her to
the man. (Genesis 2:21–22)

God fashioned Eve and custom-made her for Adam. By taking that rib from Adam and building an entire woman from that rib, God performed the first transplant surgery in history.

God believed in *hands-on* love when he made Adam and Eve. Because of God's love, God gave life to both Adam and Eve. God, the first farmer, planted all the trees. He raised livestock when he made all the animals. God gave Adam and Eve all the green plants and trees for food. He put Adam in charge of cultivating the trees. He put Adam in charge of attending to the animals. God gave life and love to Adam and Eve. So one more time, let me ask, does it make sense to fear God?

You probably said to yourself, "No, but in this case, Adam and Eve disobeyed God. So it makes sense to fear God now." That might be true, but it is also true that guilt, shame, and fear can cause you to change the way you think about things. Fear, when mixed with guilt and shame, can make you avoid people who love you. Because you are ashamed of yourself for what you have done, you do not want them to find out.

Adam and Eve were afraid of God who had given them life. They were afraid of God, who showed them love. Instead of embracing thousands of trees with gratitude, they pursued the one tree that God did not want them to have. God told them the tree of the knowledge of good and evil would kill them. And God wanted them to live.

You have probably noticed that sin is not logical. It does not make sense. When we sin we always harm ourselves or we harm someone who loves us.

Sin damaged the relationship Adam and Eve had with God. Even though they knew God loved them, sin now clouded their ability to think logically. Sin confused them. Instead of knowing God loved them and feeling secure in his love, after they sinned, they avoided God. They hid from him. They feared him. Altogether, the guilt, the shame, and the fear mixed up in their souls changed what they believed about God. And it changed what they believed about themselves.

I want to be completely clear about this. God had not changed. God still loved Adam and Eve. He still wanted to be with them. Adam and Eve had changed. They no longer wanted to be with God. They no longer embraced and received God's love.

Sin causes us to harm ourselves and to harm one another. Sin always damages our relationships. We choose to sin. We choose to harm ourselves.

God created us. He knows better than anyone what is best for us. So the Bible teaches us things like "Be honest with one another," "Be loyal to your family and to your friends," "Rest when it is time to rest," "Respect one another," "Listen closely to each other so you will understand one another," and "Love each other."

Sin wants us to be selfish. Sin wants us to be impatient with each other, to lie to one another, and to use each other as objects instead of as friends. Sin tries to hurt everything and everyone important to us. So when Adam and Eve sinned, they knew they had hurt their relationship with each other. They knew they had hurt their friendship with God.

The tree of the knowledge of good and evil promised a special knowledge. Adam and Eve discovered that special knowledge. Before they sinned, they did not experience guilt, shame, and fear. After they sinned, guilt, shame, and fear overflowed their hearts and souls. And they knew something else. They knew what it felt like to regret a decision.

CHAPTER 5

Sin Passed Down From
Parents to Children

Just like on other days, one day God came to the garden to spend some time with Adam and Eve. He enjoyed them. He loved them. So he came to the garden, but he could not find them. At that time, he yelled out for Adam, "Where are you?" (Genesis 3:9), and he listened for the response.

Adam replied by telling God that he had learned that he was naked and that he was afraid, so he hid himself from God (Genesis 3:10). God asked a couple of additional questions: "Who told you that you were naked? Have you eaten from the tree of which I commanded you not to eat?" (Genesis 3:11). God asked fair questions, but God could tell already that something had changed. Adam and Eve had not greeted him with joy and love. It seemed, they even tried to avoid him.

Sin seemed to take a life all its own with Adam and Eve. Sin seemed to pull them away from God. They no longer looked for ways to be with God. Instead, they looked for ways to hide from him or to avoid him. In addition to their fear of God, sin changed Adam's heart toward God and sin changed Eve's heart toward God. They no longer wanted to be with God.

When Adam answered God's questions, he chose to deflect attention from himself. He avoided telling God the truth. Actually, he did two things.

First, Adam chose to avoid responsibility. Second, Adam chose to blame Eve. Adam had made a decision to disobey God. Adam had

26

made a decision not to believe God. He had chosen to eat the fruit that God had told him not to eat. And with all these choices Adam made, he then tried to avoid responsibility for all his choices. He tried to say that what he had decided to do wasn't his fault: "The man said, 'The woman whom You gave to be with me, she gave me from the tree, and I ate'" (Genesis 3:12).

God had given Adam and Eve the authority to make all their own decisions. God had given them the power of a free choice; we call it free will. Adam had exercised that authority and had made his choice. But after God asked him about his choice, he blamed someone else. Did you notice that he blamed Eve (Genesis 3:12)?

For many generations, Adam and Eve have passed down the sin nature, even all the way to you and to me. Because of this, sin affects us in numerous ways. One way sin affects us is it clouds our thinking and we blame others for our problems even when our problems come because of our decisions.

Do you ever blame your brother or your sister for the mess in the bathroom or in the kitchen? Do you ever lie to your mom or dad or teacher by not taking responsibility for your decisions?

Adam told God that Eve had forced him to eat the fruit. Adam went so far as even to blame God for giving Eve to him (Genesis 3:12). Can you imagine that for a moment? God asked Adam, "Did you eat from the forbidden tree?" Adam replied, "Eve made me do it and you gave her to me. So it's really your fault."

Adam was very afraid that God would punish him. Without realizing it, the very worst thing that happened to Adam when he ate the forbidden fruit was not guilt, shame, and fear. The worst thing was that Adam became a coward in his heart and in his soul.

Adam lied to God. Lying and deception come out of a coward's heart. Adam had become a coward. Dishonesty, deception, and lying are all ways that a coward communicates.

Honesty is an expression of courage. Meeting our responsibilities is an expression of courage. Honesty and meeting our responsibilities come out of a courageous heart.

Adam was showing all the symptoms of sin. He blamed others for the problems that came from his own decisions. He avoided responsibility. He was afraid. He lied and deceived. And he felt guilty and ashamed. Within his heart, sin had turned Adam into a coward.

Well, God wanted some answers from Adam. It was clear to God that Adam and Eve understood things differently now. They understood they had a problem being naked even though being naked was not a problem before. Because of their fear of God, they ran away from him. They had never run away before. They had never feared God before.

God knew that the only thing that would change their point of view was if they had eaten from the tree of the knowledge of good and evil. They no longer knew evil by observing it from a distance. They now experienced evil because it lived within them. And the evil seemed to take on a life of its own.

In the Bible, we see a picture of evil and we see sin as a predator. Adam and Eve began to have children. They had two boys first. They named the oldest son Cain, and the next one they named Abel (Genesis 4:1–2). The Bible does not record anything about Cain and Abel until they are grown men.

The Bible records for us that Cain grew grain on his farm and Abel grew animals. One day Abel brought an animal to God and prepared to sacrifice it to God. Cain brought a basket full of grain from his farm as his sacrifice.

> So it came about in the course of time that
> Cain brought an offering to the LORD of the fruit
> of the ground. Abel, on his part also brought of
> the firstlings of his flock and of their fat portions.
> (Genesis 4:3–4)

When God told Cain that Cain needed to offer a different sacrifice, God knew Cain understood two things already. We will cover these in more detail in the next chapter, but let's look at them a little bit right now.

Cain understood that offering grain, a plant, was not an acceptable sacrifice. Cain knew that God had set the first example, the precedent. God required blood for the sacrifice, which we cannot get from a plant. Cain's parents, Adam and Eve, tried to use fig leaves to *cover* their sin: "And they sewed fig leaves together and made themselves loin coverings" (Genesis 3:7).

God's solution was to sacrifice the animal: "The LORD God made garments of skin for Adam and his wife, and clothed them" (Genesis 3:21). Cain knew that God required blood for the sacrifice, and Cain tried to ignore that. Cain wanted to do it his way instead of doing it according to God's design.

In his love and grace, God reminded Cain about the requirement of blood whenever he offers a substitute sacrifice for himself. God will not accept plants as acceptable substitutes. Cain must substitute an animal. The animal has to bleed. Blood is necessary for a sacrifice just as God had demonstrated by killing an animal as a sacrifice for Adam and Eve. Again, we will cover this in more detail in the next chapter.

God could also see into Cain's heart and soul. He could see that Cain did not want to obey God. So God gave Cain a mental image, a picture for his imagination, so that Cain would remember forever the way sin works. God said, "Sin is crouching at the door and its desire is for you, but you must master it" (Genesis 4:7).

God gave Cain the image of sin as a predator. Sin is a predator. Sin stalks us. It crouches, waiting for just the right moment to pounce and harm us. Sin wants to kill us. That explains why God wanted Adam and Eve to avoid sin altogether, but they invited it into their bodies and souls.

Because Adam and Eve invited sin into their bodies and souls, their children inherit that wickedness. Every generation that came after Adam and Eve inherited this evil sin in our hearts. The Bible records for us that our hearts are "deceitfully wicked" (Jeremiah 17:9) and that only God can cleanse our hearts from sin.

How does God cleanse our hearts of the sin that now lives within us? Let's take a closer look at what happened that day when God came looking for Adam and Eve. Please remember that Adam and Eve tried to cover themselves with fig leaves, but God had a different plan. God had a better plan.

CHAPTER 6
God Created Grace

God had told Adam that the day he ate from the tree of the knowledge of good and evil, he would die.

> From any tree of the garden you may eat
> freely; but from the tree of the knowledge of good
> and evil you shall not eat, for in the day that you
> eat from it you will surely die. (Genesis 2:16–17)

If Adam ate from that tree, he would die that very day, but Adam and Eve did eat from that tree and they did not die that day. So I am very curious. Why did Adam and Eve not die after God said they would?

Some people believe that Adam and Eve began to die or that they died spiritually. That's a fancy way of saying that Adam and Eve might die later but not on the day they sinned. In other words, did God change his mind? Did he lie? What happened?

When we read a little further into the story, we learn that God made clothing for Adam and Eve on that day: "The Lord God made garments of skin for Adam and his wife, and clothed them" (Genesis 3:21). The Bible tells us that God made garments of skin as clothing for Adam and Eve. He killed an animal and used the hide of the animal to make the clothing for Adam and Eve.

You might have read that many people did this hundreds of years ago all over the world. They would kill a deer or a cow or maybe a buffalo, and they would use the skin to make pants and coats. Well,

God killed an animal that day and performed the first work as a tailor when he sewed the skin together to make clothing for Adam and Eve.

At first glance, that might not seem important, but it is possibly the most important part of the entire story. It is so important that God made the clothing for Adam and Eve that I named this book after that event. So, please read carefully.

God had made a promise to Adam. On the day Adam sinned, Adam would die (Genesis 2:17). Sin is anything we do that disobeys God, anything that harms ourselves, anything that harms our friendships, and anything that harms our relationship with God. Adam did disobey God. So Adam should have died.

The punishment for sin is death: "The soul who sins will die" (Ezekiel 18:4), and "For the wages of sin is death" (Romans 6:23). God made that rule. Every person who ever sins should die. You sin. I sin. Every person has sinned, except one, and we will look at him in this chapter. Every person should die because of his or her sin. That is the rule God has made for every person.

Instead of dying on that day, Adam and Eve continued to live because on that day God created grace. He sat back on his throne and began to think about what he needed to do. He tried to imagine different ways to fix this problem that Adam and Eve had caused. He thought, "What if they go ahead and die?" Then he realized he did not want that to happen.

God loved Adam and Eve, so God used his creative imagination and came up with another plan. He killed the animal, and he made skins to cover their sin. That day, God decided to use an animal as a substitute for Adam and Eve. God decided that the substitute animal would pay the penalty of death for Adam and Eve. Instead of Adam and Eve dying, God decided to substitute an animal to die for them.

We do not know if the animal was an antelope or a yak or a hippopotamus or maybe a zebra. We just do not know. It had to be big enough to provide clothing to cover both Adam and Eve. Even though Adam and Eve had tried to cover themselves with fig leaves, God decided that an animal's skin was better.

God found an animal big enough to provide clothing for both Adam and Eve. The Bible does not tell us which animal. It probably was not an ostrich or an alligator. God picked a large animal, large enough to have skin to cover both Adam and Eve. The Bible records that God made garments from animal skin for Adam and Eve (Genesis 3:21).

God made a decision that day. He decided to kill the animal instead of making Adam and Eve die that day.

That day God created grace. Grace is the unearned love of God. Adam and Eve had earned death, but God gave them life. He gave them unearned love and life. In creating that grace, God required three things. Let's look closely at each one of them.

God had told Adam that on the day you eat from the tree of the knowledge of good and evil you will die (Genesis 2:17). Instead of requiring Adam and Eve to die, God substituted an animal. On the day Adam and Eve ate from the tree, the animal died and it died as a substitute for Adam and Eve.

The Bible teaches us that Jesus Christ died as our substitute when he died on the cross. He died to meet God's requirement that those who sin should die. Jesus never sinned, so he could die for your sins instead of you dying for your sins. Instead of God making us die for our own sins, he made Jesus die for the sins of everyone in the world. To provide what the Bible calls grace, God chose a substitute for you and for me, and that substitute was Jesus.

When Adam and Eve tried to fix their sin themselves, they gathered fig leaves and sewed them together. For God to satisfy his justice, these plants chosen by Adam and Eve were not enough. Plants do not bleed when they die. The sacrifice must include blood, and not just a little blood. It had to include all the blood of the person who had sinned.

When God substituted the animal, all the blood of the animal was a requirement. The animal had to bleed. I know this might seem nasty to you and to me, and God does not explain it. We simply have to figure it out by looking closely at the story.

On the cross of Calvary, Jesus Christ bled to death. Between the beatings and his crucifixion, Jesus lost all his blood that day.

Medical doctors tell us about all the different ways Jesus suffered and about all the different ways the soldiers beat him and caused him to bleed. The Bible teaches us that the blood of Jesus cleanses us from all our sins.

> You were not redeemed with perishable things like silver or gold from your futile way of life inherited from your forefathers, but with precious blood, as of a lamb unblemished and spotless, the blood of Christ. (1 Peter 1:18–19)

> If we walk in the light as He Himself is in the Light, we have fellowship with one another, and the blood of Jesus His Son cleanses us from all sin. (1 John 1:7)

The Bible teaches us that without the shedding of blood, there is no forgiveness of sins (Hebrews 9:22).

When Adam and Eve needed God's grace to cover their sins, God sacrificed the animal. God did not tell Adam to do it. Adam could not take credit for killing the animal because Adam did not kill the animal. God did not ask an angel to kill the animal for Adam and Eve. God killed the animal. God made the sacrifice himself.

On the cross, the Bible teaches us that Jesus was the Lamb of God: "Behold, the Lamb of God who takes away the sin of the world" (John 1:29). Jesus was not the lamb offered by a group of human beings. So, the Bible teaches that in some way God sacrificed Jesus for your sins and for mine. The nation of Israel did not sacrifice Jesus. God did. The world did not sacrifice Jesus. Somehow, God sacrificed Jesus for you and for me.

We can read about Jesus dying on the cross for you and for me in the Gospel of Matthew, in the Gospel of Mark, in the Gospel of Luke, and in the Gospel of John. We can read about Jesus bleeding and about his death.

I think it is amazing that God began to offer his grace to Adam and to Eve in the garden of Eden, and I think it is amazing that God offers his grace completely to you and to me with Jesus dying on the cross. God offers us complete grace.

In the garden of Eden, the substitute was an animal. For all time and for every person, the all-time substitute is Jesus. In the garden of Eden, God killed an animal and its blood paid the penalty for Adam and Eve's sin. At Calvary, Jesus bled and died, and his blood pays the penalty for the sins of every person who ever lived in the whole world. In the garden of Eden, God killed the animal as the sacrifice for Adam and Eve. On the cross, Jesus was the Lamb of God with God doing the work to take away your sins and my sins.

When Adam and Eve sinned, they began to experience guilt, shame, and fear. They became cowards. When you and I ask Jesus to enter our hearts, he replaces the guilt, shame, and fear with peace, joy, and hope: "Now may the God of hope fill you with all joy and peace in believing, so that you will abound in hope" (Romans 15:13).

Jesus changes us from being cowards who stay away from God to being courageous boys who are attracted to God and courageous girls who are attracted to God. Jesus forgives us, and Jesus changes us on the inside. Once we are changed on the inside from cowardly to courageous, then the outside changes also. We become honest. We become responsible. We become compassionate.

That day in the garden of Eden, God created grace. God designed the plan for sacrificing animals as substitutes. God used this design for many years so that people could receive mercy and grace when they sinned. And when Jesus came to earth, Jesus told us that he did not come to stop the sacrifices. He did not come to stop the grace of God. He came to complete the grace of God: "Do not think that I came to abolish the Law or the Prophets; I did not come to abolish but to fulfill" (Matthew 5:17).

What God had started and offered only partially in the garden of Eden, Jesus came to complete. Jesus completed the grace that God had created in the garden of Eden.

Grace is God's love and mercy. We cannot earn God's love and grace. We have earned judgment and death, but God figured out a way to give us mercy and grace. This is because God loves us for all eternity.

Please take a few minutes right now and pray. Bow your head and thank God for his grace. Use this next paragraph to guide you.

Thank God for sending Jesus as a substitute for your death so that you can live forever with him in heaven. Thank God for Jesus bleeding and dying for you so that you can live for him on earth right here and right now. Ask God to forgive you of all those sins you have done and ask Jesus to live in your heart. Tell God that you want to live your life for him, in a way that honors him. Then thank God for forgiving you of your sins.

Make sure you tell your mother or your father or whoever takes care of you that you have asked Jesus to come into your heart. Make sure you tell that person that you have decided to live your life to honor Jesus.

CHAPTER 7
God Created Us in His Image

The question comes up, why did God offer salvation for Adam and Eve but not for Satan and the angels? The fast answer is that God created Adam and Eve in his image. God set Adam and Eve apart from all the rest of creation. God created them in his own image: "God created man in His own image, in the image of God He created him; male and female He created them" (Genesis 1:27).

Genesis records for us that God created the world and everything in it. When God did that, he decided to make human beings different from plants and animals. He created Adam and Eve differently than the sun and the stars. He even created humanity differently than the angels.

The angels are a different form of beings. When we die and go to heaven, we do not become angels. We have already looked a little at God creating the angels, specifically at Lucifer who was one of the archangels along with Gabriel and Michael. After Michael threw Lucifer out of heaven, Lucifer's name was changed to Satan or the devil. We do not know how many angels God created. We do not know much about the different styles or the different types of angels. Very few details are given about the angels.

In Genesis, we can read how Jacob had a dream and saw the angels going up a ladder and going down the same ladder: "He had a dream, and behold, a ladder was set on the earth with its top reaching to heaven; and behold, the angels of God were ascending and descending on it" (Genesis 28:10–17). God stood at the top of the ladder. The bottom of the ladder stood on the earth, and the top of the ladder rested against the edge of heaven.

The first two chapters of Job record that the angels stand in line waiting to give God a report on their previous assignments and to get another assignment from God: "Now there was a day when the sons of God came to present themselves before the Lord, and Satan also came among them" (Job 1:6), and "Again there was a day when the sons of God came to present themselves before the Lord, and Satan also came among them to present himself before the Lord" (Job 2:1). The first chapter of Hebrews finishes by asking us a question about the angels: "Are they not all ministering spirits sent out to render service for the sake of those who will inherit salvation?" (Hebrews 1:14).

The Bible does not tell us much about the appearance of the angels. The Bible does not tell us much about their skin color or their tone of voice. The Bible does not tell us if they are tall or short, fat or thin. What the Bible does tell us from these three passages in Genesis, Job, and Hebrews is that the angels work for God to help human beings.

This is one of the most significant differences between the angels and us. The angels help you and me. We do not help them. Angels and humans are different. Humans are created in the image of God. Angels are not. This is one of the most significant points about being created in the image of God, our value. God values us greatly, even more than the angels. We will return to this in a little while.

What does it mean to be created in the image of God? Does it mean that we have the same eye color as God? Does it mean that God is a boy or a girl? Does it mean that God is tall or short, fat or thin? Well, you can use your imagination to think about many things about God. Here are four things that the Bible includes when it teaches us that you and I are created in the image of God.

First, God created you with the ability to plan ahead. The fancy word for that is *forethought*. You can plan which streets you want to take to get to the grocery store or to get to the mall. You can plan ahead to go different ways home from school each day of the week. God has given you the ability of forethought, thinking ahead, the ability to plan. Rocks do not have this skill or ability. Trees and flowers do not have this ability. Butterflies, salamanders, sharks, and chimpanzees do not have the ability to think in advance and then decide which option they prefer.

You have the ability to look in the refrigerator and decide which food you prefer to eat tonight and which food you will wait to eat tomorrow. You can decide to boil or fry an egg. You can decide to walk to the bathroom backward or walk sideways and try to figure out in advance the quicker way. Birds and lizards do not have the ability of forethought. Angels seem to share this ability with us, but God did not create them in his image.

Second, God also built creativity into you and me when he created us in his image. Even though spiders spin intricate webs that glisten in the sunlight with the morning dew, the individual spiders still spin specific web patterns. God seems to make every snowflake different, but that is God, not a snowy owl or a reindeer. Animals do not enjoy the creativity we humans possess all because God did not create them in his image.

This creativity in you and me has its limits. We cannot create like God created. We cannot bring things into existence like God did. We can only take what already exists and use our creativity to come up with new combinations.

Even though we have only three primary colors—red, blue, and yellow—we can use our creativity to come up with thousands of different combinations for thousands of different colors. We can discover things like the time Sir Isaac Newton discovered gravity or when in 1752 Benjamin Franklin flew a kite with a key attached to the string hoping to attract a lightning bolt and learn a little more about electricity. Gravity and electricity had existed since God created the world, but someone had to discover them and learn how to use them to help us with our lives.

We can use our creativity to make new combinations, but only God can create. Only God can bring something into existence. When God created us in his image, he included creativity.

Third, when God created us in his image, he included our free will. That's the fancy way of saying you get to make your own choices. God thought about staying in control forcing everyone to love and obey him, but he realized it really doesn't count if he makes us obey him or if he makes us love him.

This free will might be the most important part of growing up. By making our own decisions we learn how to accept more responsibility. Maybe you learn to make your bed every day. Then after you have made your bed every day for a month, your mom tells you that you have shown enough responsibility and that you will now have to clean your entire room every Saturday. This is not punishment. These are step by step lessons learning how to develop responsibility.

By using your free will, you can build your responsibility. After you have cleaned your room every Saturday for two entire months, your mom might tell you that you have learned enough about responsibility to get a puppy.

Did you notice your mom was trying to build you up by starting small? You started by making your bed. Then you learned to make your bed on your own initiative. After that, you cleaned your room, and again you learned to clean it without being told to do so.

You need to do these steps consistently and without your mom telling you over and over again. Then with that puppy, you learn how to make sure she has food and water every day. You learn how to give her a bath. And you learn how to clean up her messes. In addition to playing with your new puppy and holding her, you learn a higher level of responsibility by taking care of her.

If your mom were to do this, she would help you to use your free will to develop your responsibility. As she teaches you, you cooperate and learn. You choose to make your bed. You choose to remember to make your bed so that your mom doesn't have to remind you. Then you choose to clean up your room. Then you choose to remember to clean up your room without your mom telling you to do so.

Then you discover a couple of things about combining free will with forethought. You discover that you can clean up your room after school on Friday so that you can play all day Saturday. After that point, you notice that if you clean your room three times per week instead of only once, it actually takes less time in total. It takes you ten minutes for each of the three different times, or it takes you one hour on Saturday.

So you start to keep your room clean because you discover that keeping it tidy takes less time and less work than it does to clean it entirely once per week. Then your mom notices that you have become responsible enough to start learning how to take care of a puppy. I hope this step-by-step progression makes sense to you. It is your free will in action that God gave you when he created you in his image.

We can also see this God-given free will as you make other choices. You will choose to drink alcohol or not. You will choose to smoke cigarettes or Vape or not. You will choose to experiment with drugs or not. You will choose to have sex before marriage or not. You will choose to use profanity or not. You will choose to watch things on TV or on the Internet that you are not allowed to watch or not. You will choose to eat healthy food or junk food. You will choose to bathe daily or not or to brush your teeth daily or not. You will choose to respect your teachers or not. God has given you this free will. By creating you in his image, God gave you a powerful tool in this free will. I hope and pray that you learn to use it wisely.

Let's look at your free will a little longer. Every decision you make with your free will has automatic consequences. If you choose to sit on the sofa, you automatically do not stand in the kitchen. If you choose to watch a movie on TV, you automatically do not ride a bicycle. Every decision you make has automatic consequences. Let me tell you two stories to help you understand these consequences.

Many teachers liked and respected Susan. She earned good grades and she played on the basketball team at school. During one game, the other team had two players who kept saying mean things to Susan. My children call that "smack talk." Susan tried to stay focused and concentrate on winning the game. One of the other players pushed her. Susan stayed focused. The other player elbowed Susan on the side of her head. Susan turned around and punched that second player. The referee threw both Susan and her opponent out of the ball game. What are the automatic consequences?

Susan was thrown out of the ballgame, but that was not an automatic consequence. That was a chosen consequence, chosen by the referee. The automatic consequence came the next week during the next game when another player started to pick on Susan. Her coach pulled her out of the game and sat her on the bench because the coach believed Susan could no longer control her temper. The coach did not choose to no longer trust Susan to stay focused. It was an automatic consequence. The coach lost some confidence in Susan as a reliable player.

Another example is the day when Maria's dad got home late from a meeting at work. When he got home, he discovered that Maria had washed all the dishes, dried them, and put them away. She had cleaned the kitchen countertops. She had even folded the towels in the laundry basket. When her dad asked her what was going on, Maria replied, "I knew you would get home late and be tired. So I thought I would help." What are the automatic consequences of Maria's decisions?

Her dad did not choose to be happy or grateful. He felt happy and grateful automatically. He thanked Maria for her help. He told her that he recognized she was growing up and learning more responsibility. He realized she was learning to consider other people, to consider their feelings, to consider what they want or don't want. He respected Maria and trusted her a little more, not because he chose to do so. The added respect and trust were automatic.

By using our free will, we can build our courage. We can build our responsibility. We can build our compassion. We can build our honesty. We can make intentional efforts to build or develop ourselves to be the person God dreams for us to be. We can cooperate with God by planning ahead and by using our free will.

Even though there are several points to God creating us in his image, and we have covered three of them, let's return now to our earlier discussion about our value. Because God created us in his image, we have more value than the rocks and the trees, and more value than the oceans and the animals. We even have more value than the angels.

Along with Satan, when the angels sinned, God created hell for them: "Then He will also say to those on His left, 'depart from Me, accursed ones, into the eternal fire which has been prepared for the devil and his angels'" (Matthew 25:41). When Adam and Eve sinned,

God began to work out a plan that led to their salvation and to the salvation of the entire world through Jesus Christ.

In the previous chapter we looked at God creating grace. This difference in value between the angels and humans is that God had created Adam and Eve in his image. When the angels sinned, God threw them out of heaven. When humans sinned, God established the plan to bring us into heaven. To help us understand how much God values us, let me share with you a story that a missionary shared with me.

Many years ago, John and Sarah lived in China as missionaries. Missionaries are people who have asked Jesus to live in their hearts. Missionaries have asked Jesus to forgive their sins. Missionaries have thanked God for his forgiveness and for the love that he gives us when we give our hearts to Jesus to live for him. Missionaries go to other nations to teach people about Jesus and about his love for them.

As John walked down the street one day in Canton, China, he remembered that the next day he and Sarah would celebrate their wedding anniversary. His wife, Sarah, would want a present for their anniversary. They did not have a lot of money, but John wanted to get an anniversary gift for Sarah. So he went into a little shop hoping to find something to purchase for her.

As he looked around, he spotted a necklace made up of blue beads, Sarah's favorite color. John asked the store owner the price of the necklace. The store owner told John he would accept $5 for the necklace. John did not have a lot of money, but he did have that much with him. So he dug through his pockets and gathered up the money and gave it to the store owner. John took the necklace of blue beads and walked home. He wrapped the beads in an old newspaper and waited for the next day to present the necklace to Sarah.

Soon after breakfast, John invited Sarah back to the table and gave her the necklace. Sarah opened the newspaper wrapping and held the blue beads. She just looked at the blue beads and began to smile. She noticed some scratches, but she figured out quickly that they did not have a lot of money and that John probably had spent money intended for food so she could have that necklace. With tears of joy, she hugged John and had him help her put on the necklace. She wanted to wear the pretty blue beads.

A couple of years went by. John and Sarah returned to the United States. As missionaries, they would come to the United States in order to travel to many churches to ask people to support their mission work with prayers. They would tell stories of their work in China and ask people if they would help them financially. Usually each church had two or three families who would help. This traveling from church to church usually took as long as a year for John and Sarah.

One day, while in New York, Sarah mentioned to John that the clasp on her blue bead necklace had broken. She asked him if he would take it to a jewelry store to have it repaired. The necklace had become her favorite piece of jewelry. Not only was blue her favorite color, but the beads were her favorite shade of blue. So John looked around for a jewelry store and found Tiffany's, a famous world-class jewelry store.

When John entered Tiffany's, he located a sales clerk who took the necklace and began to examine it. He assured John that he could fix the clasp in a few minutes. Soon after the clerk went to the back of the store, John heard a commotion coming from the back of the store. A man wearing a suit came out from the back asking if John owned the blue bead necklace. John assured him that he was the owner.

The man introduced himself as Mr. Tiffany, the owner of the store, and asked John to tell him where he found that necklace. John told him all about China and serving as a missionary. John told him about the small shop and the shop owner. And about that time in the story, Mr. Tiffany asked John if he would accept $50,000 for the necklace.

This offer shocked John, and John did not know what to say. He asked for the necklace and left the store. He walked around for a few minutes knowing that $50,000 would pay for the next twenty years of ministry in China. He also knew the necklace had great sentimental value for his wife, but she would sell it in order to pay for their ministry.

John did not want to ask his wife to part with her favorite piece of jewelry. She had worn it often and had enjoyed wearing it. She liked the way it sparkled. She overlooked the scratches. Each time she put it on, she remembered how John had sacrificed a week's worth of food for himself so that she could have a pretty necklace to wear. He remembered all this, and he decided to go back to Tiffany's.

When John entered the store, Mr. Tiffany stood in the showroom helping another customer. When he saw John, he excused himself and came over to John and said, "I'll increase my offer to $75,000." John just stared at him for a moment. Then John asked, "Please tell me why you want to spend $75,000 on a scratched-up necklace of blue beads that cost me $5."

Mr. Tiffany reached into his pocket and took out his eyepiece to examine the necklace. He handed it to John and told him to hold the necklace up toward the light and look at the beads. When John held it up, also holding the eyepiece to his eye, he could see sparkles and details he had never seen before. The beads were wonderfully beautiful. Mr. Tiffany then told John, "Look at the engravings. Do you see it is the same on each stone?" John saw a specific design on each bead. Previously, he thought these were scratches, but now he could tell it was an engraved design.

Mr. Tiffany continued, "When Napoleon had finished the French Revolution and was ready to return home, he wanted to take a gift to his beloved Josephine. Those of us in the jewelry business have heard about this necklace. This is the necklace Napoleon had made for Josephine. There is an engraving on many of the stones. These are not beads. These are rare blue pearls. This is the blue pearl necklace Napoleon had made for Josephine. It is a priceless piece of history."

Now, let's get back to the explanation about God creating us in his own image. Many times we get "scratched" or have our feelings hurt. Sometimes people can harm us in nasty or insulting ways, and even in degrading ways. Sometimes people can hurt us all the way to our hearts and souls. Because we can get hurt like that, we think we are useless and are not valuable. We think less of ourselves.

Sometimes we are ashamed of ourselves even though it was another person who harmed us. We did nothing wrong. Someone else harmed us, but we think less of ourselves because of it.

We think sometimes that we should just throw away ourselves like a piece of old worthless everyday jewelry. But then God looks at us with his special eyesight. He looks deep inside and sees that he created us. He sees his image engraved on our souls. God realizes that we are not throwaway junk. God knows that we have incredible value because he does not make junk. He makes treasures. We are worth more than anyone could ever pay. We are priceless because God has created us in his image.

We are a priceless part of God's entire creation and he never wants to lose us, so he built a plan to save us. He built a plan to buy us back from sin and from death. God has to buy us back because Adam and Eve sold us into sin and into death. Because of God's incredible love and mercy for you and for me, he sacrificed his only Son, Jesus Christ.

Just like the way God substituted an animal for Adam and Eve in the garden of Eden, God substituted Jesus for you and for me. Just like Adam and Eve tried to fix their sin by covering themselves with fig leaves, many times you and I try to fix our problem of sin by doing good things. We think and hope that maybe God will like the good things and overlook the bad things we have done. We try to balance out the bad with the good.

We think that maybe our good works and feelings of regret will be enough. But God knew that because someone had to die, they had to lose all their blood. Just like the animal that lost its blood in the garden of Eden, Jesus lost all his blood on the cross for you and for me. Our good works do not take away our sin. The blood of Jesus takes away our sin.

God offered Jesus for us. God did not ask someone else to sacrifice Jesus. When John the Baptist introduced Jesus to the crowd at the Jordan River, he called Jesus "the Lamb of God who takes away the sin of the world" (John 1:29). Jesus was not the sacrificed lamb of Israel. He was not the sacrificed lamb of you and me. Jesus was the sacrificed Lamb of God. God gave Jesus. God sacrificed Jesus because God values you and me that much.

All across the world, most people who give their lives to Jesus do so before their fourteenth birthday. You might be reading this book before your fourteenth birthday. Regardless of your age, you can experience Jesus in your own heart right now.

If you want to experience Jesus in your own heart, take some time right now and pray to God in your own words thanking God for substituting Jesus for you. Thank Jesus for his blood that washes away your sins. Thank Jesus for forgiving you of your sins. Ask Jesus to live in your heart and tell him that you will live your life trusting him and obeying him.

CHAPTER 8

God's Creation Is Good and Complete

In the book of Genesis, God reveals to us that the number seven (7) is the number of completion. God created the world in seven days. Just like putting together a puzzle or building a model, God put the universe together piece by piece. He worked hard for six days, and the Bible records for us that he rested on the seventh day.

Six times, God looked at what he had created and announced, "It is good" (Genesis 1:4, 1:10, 1:12, 1:18, 1:21, 1:25) with the seventh time stating, "It is very good" (Genesis 1:31). When God looked at the Atlantic Ocean, the Himalayan Mountains, and the Serengeti Plains of Africa, he said all of it was good. When he looked at the rings around Saturn, the asteroid field between Mars and Jupiter, Orion's belt, and our sun, he again said it all was good. When God looked at the chameleon, the giant squid, and the Andean condor, he said, "It is good." After he created Adam and Eve, he sat back on his throne, looked over the entire universe together, grinned from ear to ear, and announced for the seventh time, "It is very good."

In those early chapters of Genesis the word *create* is used seven times (Genesis 1:1, 1:21, 1:27, 2:3, 2:4). This word is used only for God taking action. You and I can invent something or make something. We can take existing materials and use our imaginations to put them together in a new way, but only God can create. Only God can bring something into existence when it did not exist just a minute earlier. The Bible never uses the word *create* for the activity of any human. To create is something only God can do.

God created the heavens and the earth. We don't know a whole lot about heaven. The Bible tells us that it is a wonderful place. The

47

Bible tells us that God created heaven in one day but that Jesus has been busy for over two thousand years getting a special area of heaven ready just for you. The Bible tells us that in heaven we will not be sad. We will not cry. We will have a reunion with our family members and friends who have died.

While Benny and his dad fished in the river beside the factory, Benny's dad had a heart attack and later died. Benny will see his dad again.

When Briseeka came home from school on Friday excited to learn how to bake cookies, she learned her grandmother had fallen down the stairs. Her grandmother was taken to the hospital and died. Briseeka will get to bake cookies with her grandmother in heaven someday.

Before Samantha's best friend, Shonda, died of cancer they played with dolls and sang songs. When Samantha gets to heaven, she and Shonda will play and sing again. In heaven, God has horses we can ride. We will run and dance, climb trees, swim in rivers, and worship God.

The Bible also records that God created all the fish and all the birds. The great blue whale is the largest animal that has ever lived weighing as much as 190 tons and stretching as much as 98 feet long. Mackerels swim in schools with so many fish the school can stretch as far as 20 miles. Seahorses are the slowest-swimming fish, and unlike other fish, the male gives birth to the babies. An electric eel can generate over 850 volts and 1 ampere of electric power. Can you come up with other examples of God's imagination in creating the fish and the animals that live in the oceans, seas, and rivers?

Have you ever watched a thousand sparrows fly together? They fly with precision and harmony in motion. Canada geese fly in a V formation so that when one goose flaps its wings pushing the air down, that air comes back up under the wings of the next goose. This helps them to fly up to 70 percent farther than they could fly alone. The hummingbird can fly backward and the peregrine falcon can dive toward its prey at 200 miles per hour. The eagle can fly so high it can soar even above a thunderstorm. The roadrunner can run up to 20 miles per hour while the ostrich can run 30 miles per hour. The owls can rotate their heads 270 degrees. With all these differences and a thousand more, the Bible records that God used his imagination to create all the birds.

The first two chapters of the Bible record seven times that God created something, that God brought something into existence. The Bible uses the word create three times when it talks specifically about God creating Adam and Eve. By repeating this three times, the Bible emphasizes the point that God created Adam and Eve instead of making them. God gave them his undivided attention: "God *created* man in His own image. In the image of God He *created* him; male and female He *created* them" (Genesis 1:27; italics added).

At first, the word *man* is used to mean mankind or humanity. Then the Bible clarifies exactly that God created man in his image and God created woman in his image. Don't let anyone fool you into thinking that you have to have a boyfriend or a girlfriend to be complete. You are complete by yourself because God created you in his image.

By creating you in his image, God gave you great worth and purpose. We all have ways to contribute to the world. To Adam and Eve, God gave the entire garden of Eden to cultivate it, care for it, and help it to thrive. He has created you uniquely to benefit your family, to benefit your community, and even to benefit the world.

The Bible records for us that God announced six times that the world he created was good, and on the seventh time, he said, "It was very good" (Genesis 1:31). He created everything beautiful. Have you ever noticed a sunset with pink clouds, orange clouds, and red clouds stretched across the sky like cotton candy? He makes the highest mountain peaks covering them with snow. And then he made the music.

The music started with the flow of a stream over the rocks or maybe the sound of tree limbs full of leaves brushing against each other in the breeze. God added in the songs of the mourning doves calling to one another across the meadow. He blended in the coyotes and the wolves howling with the nightingales and the loons singing to the sunset. And somewhere Adam learned to play percussion by taking a stick and hitting a hollow tree.

If you have taken music lessons, you know that percussion instruments involve hitting a surface with a stick or a mallet. Woodwinds like the clarinet and saxophone have a reed that vibrates with your breath going through the tube. Brass instruments like the trumpet or trombone have a mouthpiece where you vibrate your lips together to make the sound. Stringed instruments like the violin or cello use a bow that you push and pull across the strings. All the music, every single note God created on a seven-note design.

You might have a music teacher who tells you that within music, an octave is twelve notes. When you include the sharps and flats, you get twelve notes. Some teachers will tell you that an octave is eight notes—A-B-C-D-E-F-G-A. Even though the definition of an octave might be eight notes, please notice that the first and last notes are the same note. In other words, because God created the world using the number seven as the number of completion, we can see God's touch in our music.

There are seven notes, A-B-C-D-E-F-G, and then the notes repeat. In between this seven-note structure are the places we find the sharps and the flats. C-sharp is the same as D-flat. D-sharp is the same as E-flat, and so on. God created music, and because he created it, we have discovered it is on a seven-note design.

CHAPTER 9

God Created Interdependence

When God created the universe, he created it very good, and he created the different parts to live interdependently with one another. This is a big fancy word that means two or more parts rely on each other to live. For example, with music you have the melody and the harmony interdependent with one another, relying on each other to give a full sound to the song.

When Genesis records each day of creation, we can read, "And there was evening and there was morning" (Genesis 1:5, 1:8, 1:13, 1:19, 1:23, 1:31), and then each day is identified as one day, or as a second day, or as a third day, and so on. For God, the day began with sunset. The day began with rest for the upcoming activities during the daylight hours. Still today we follow this pattern established by God by starting the new day at midnight. We start the day by resting usually.

The doctors who study people when they sleep tell us that during our deepest sleep, our brains clean themselves. Have you ever noticed the exhaust mark that appears on the road just below the exhaust pipe of a car where the car has kept running but has stayed parked?

Doctors tell us that we have a little "dirt" deposited in our brains with every brain nerve that fires. These waste products get deposited in our brains, and our brains can only clean out the waste products when we experience our deepest sleep. This prepares our brain for the next day of work and play.

God created us with interdependence between rest and activity. We need to sleep so that we can work and play effectively. Have you ever tried to work or pay attention at school when you have not slept well? It doesn't work well, does it? We need to work and we need to sleep.

When we look at the world God has created, we can recognize that God enjoys creating interdependent systems. That word means that parts of a system depend upon one another. When God created the Milky Way galaxy along with all the other galaxies in the universe, he created them interdependent with one another.

You probably have learned in science class that the planets orbit around the sun because the sun's gravitational pull draws them to itself. Why do Jupiter and Saturn stay in their orbits? Why do Earth and Mars stay in their orbits? You probably have learned the answer to these questions in science class also. Expert scientists have discovered that the gravitational pull of the other stars and the other planets counter or balance out the gravitational pull of the sun. We experience an incredible interdependent balance of gravity.

The sun pulls on the earth, and so do all the other stars and planets. The combined gravitational pulls all balance out so that the earth stays in its orbit just like Neptune and Mercury each stay in their orbits. All the stars and planets are in gravitational balance because God created these bodies within the universe to live interdependently with each other.

A little closer to home, God also used his amazing imagination when he created plants and animals to live interdependently with one another. God made the trees and the bushes, as well as the weeds and the grass, to grow out of the ground. He grew the mighty Sumaumeira trees in the Amazon Jungle, which grow to 200 feet tall and 10 feet in diameter, while also growing the giant redwood trees in California to reach 350 feet tall and 18 feet in diameter. He also grew all the trees in your neighborhood park or maybe in your own yard.

All the trees along with all the bushes and all the other plants that have green leaves breathe in carbon dioxide and breathe out oxygen. You probably have learned this in science class. You probably have learned that plants depend on animals to breathe out carbon dioxide. At the same time, animals depend on plants to breathe out oxygen.

The people who cut down trees are called loggers. They cut down trees for the wood, and then they plant younger trees to grow in their place. This maintains the balance and replenishes the trees to produce the oxygen needed by all the animals.

I hope you have noticed the interdependence between the plants and the animals. The plants breathe in carbon dioxide and breathe out oxygen. The animals breathe in oxygen and breathe out carbon dioxide. This is why God created plants and animals so quickly. They could not survive for a long time without each other. They depend upon one another for their next breath.

As humans, we also depend on plants for breathing out oxygen so we can breathe it in. We exhale carbon dioxide, which plants breathe in to survive.

All this interdependence between melody and harmony, between rest and work, balanced gravitational pulls, and the oxygen-carbon dioxide cycle can help to explain why God created the world in such a short period of time. How many more interdependent relationships can you discover within God's creation?

While you use your tremendous imagination God has given to you to look around the world, let's take a look at how God finished his creation. With yet another interdependent relationship, God finished by creating Adam and Eve. Instead of keeping them independent from one another, or even dependent upon one another, God placed them in an interdependent relationship with one another.

CHAPTER 10
God Created Marriage

God deliberately created many things opposite from one another and interdependent with one another when he created the universe. He created the heavens opposite to the earth. He created the light opposite to darkness. He created the sea opposite to the dry land. He created the sun and the moon. He created the fish and the birds. He created Adam and Eve opposite to one another and interdependent with one another.

God created Adam "to cultivate and to care for" the garden of Eden (Genesis 2:15, author's translation). This established a standing rule that God wanted Adam to cultivate and care for everything God gave to him. God wanted Adam to care for the pine tree, the red raspberries, and the jujube tree. God wanted Adam to care for the fig tree, the pineapple tree, and the flowering magnolia tree.

Even though God had created everything good, God did not believe it was good for Adam to be alone: "Then the LORD God said, 'It is not good for the man to be alone; I will make him a helper suitable for him'" (Genesis 2:18). God created all the animals and brought them to Adam so that Adam could name them. By naming the animals, Adam agreed to take care of them just like he had agreed to take care of the garden. Adam named the praying mantis and the walking stick. Adam named the penguin and the flamingo. He named the anteater and the alligator, but none of these would live as an interdependent opposite mate for Adam.

So God used his imagination again. He had Adam fall into a deep sleep (Genesis 2:21). While Adam slept, God performed that first transplant surgery taking one of Adam's ribs and building Eve from that rib.

> So the LORD God caused a deep sleep to fall
> upon the man, and he slept; then He took one of
> his ribs and closed up the flesh at that place. The
> LORD God fashioned into a woman the rib which
> He had taken from the man, and brought her to
> the man. (Genesis 2:21–22)

God fashioned Eve similar to Adam in many ways, and God fashioned Eve exactly the opposite in many ways. God created both Adam and Eve with bones and muscles and with blood and hair. They both had two eyes, two ears, two nostrils, and one mouth. These seven holes in their heads are how they observe and receive information. They see with their eyes, hear with their ears, smell with their nostrils, and taste with their mouths. Add to this the sense of touch and you have all the ways Adam and Eve could take in information and learn about their world.

God also created Adam and Eve opposite in many ways. Eve's frame was softer while Adam's frame was stronger. Eve spoke more while Adam wanted to play more. Eve used her imagination. Adam seemed to want to work. Eve seemed more ready to care for Adam than Adam seemed ready to care for Eve. Together, they made great music. Adam set the melody, and Eve filled it all in with beautiful harmony.

God had created Eve specifically for Adam. God had made all the arrangements for that first wedding. He might have escorted Eve through the grape arbor with macaws and spider monkeys perched in the surrounding trees watching the ceremony. When God presented Eve to Adam, Adam replied, "This is now bone of my bones and flesh of my flesh. She shall be called woman because she was taken out of man" (Genesis 2:23).

Then the Bible records, "For this reason a man shall leave his father and his mother, and be joined to his wife; and they shall become one flesh. And the man and his wife were both naked and were not ashamed" (Genesis 2:25).

God created the marriage between a husband and a wife to serve forever as the primary relationship on earth. God designed the marriage to be one man and one woman, one husband and one wife.

Adam and Eve had many children. Since sinfulness passed from Adam and Eve to each generation, this sinfulness has caused many people to corrupt their marriages. The Bible records for us that about five generations later, Lamech married two wives. We see the corruption of marriage with one man having more than one wife or one woman having more than one husband, a man and a woman living together without getting married, divorce, homosexuality, and other corruptions of God's design. Instead of discussing all the different ways humans have corrupted marriage, let's invest our time together to help you to understand God's design for marriage.

God did not create Eve primarily for her children Cain and Abel. God created her for Adam. Sometimes a mother will love her children more than she will love her husband or a father will love his children more than he will love his wife. These corruptions in God's design cause those families to have many difficulties. Some of those marriages end in divorce and the children cry the hardest. God wants each husband to love his wife most and each wife to love her husband most. When the husband loves his wife the most, the family is safe. When the wife loves her husband the most, the family is safe.

By loving each other the most, the parents will provide a home where the children will be safe and secure. The husband knows God wants him to keep his wife in his heart. The wife knows God wants her side by side with her husband. Those marriages will not divorce.

When Adam named Eve, he agreed to God's plan that he should always cherish Eve, honor Eve, and love Eve most of all. Adam agreed to take care of Eve just like he agreed to take care of the garden and just like he agreed to take care of the animals. God created Eve to work side by side with Adam and to honor, respect, and love him the most.

God did not take the bone from Adam's foot so that Adam would *step* on Eve and treat Eve like a servant. God did not want

Adam scolding Eve or yelling at her or harming her. God wanted Adam to cherish Eve and to treasure her above everything and above everyone else in his life.

God did not take the bone from Adam's head so that Eve would bully Adam. God wanted her to work side by side with Adam as his very best friend, always honoring him and loving him above everything and above everyone else in her life.

God used a rib from Adam so that Eve would always be held when she needed a hug. God wanted Adam to hold her close to his heart. God wanted Eve to be Adam's very best friend. God wanted Adam and Eve to trust one another and always love one another.

When Adam and Eve finished that first wedding, the Bible records that they were naked and felt no shame: "And the man and his wife were both naked and were not ashamed" (Genesis 2:25). Please notice that the Bible talks about their physical condition. They wore no clothing, and then the Bible does not say if they were cold or not. After mentioning that they were naked, the Bible then records their emotions.

The Bible gives us a hint that Adam and Eve felt no shame when God first created them. You might remember that they felt shame later when they ate fruit from the tree of the knowledge of good and evil. They felt shame when they sinned.

Adam and Eve lived a long time ago. God wanted them to enjoy their lives and marriage without any shame. Even today, God wants you to enjoy your life without shame. God wants you to enjoy a marriage someday without shame.

If you want to be married someday, you could start now learning how to respect other people and how to cherish them. You can use your free will to show respect to your teachers, classmates, and parents. You can begin praying now asking God to help you become the husband or the wife God wants you to be.

You can use your free will to ask Jesus into your heart as Savior and Lord so that you will be courageous instead of cowardly. You can use your free will to develop your responsibility, your honesty, and your compassion. If you are a boy, you can use your free will to work interdependently with God to develop you into the kind of man women want as a husband. If you are a girl, you can use your free will to work interdependently with God to develop you into the kind of woman men want as a wife.

If you are a boy, you can pray that God helps you choose a wife with the same beliefs and values that you have. If you are a girl, you can pray that God helps you choose a husband with the same beliefs and values that you have.

God has wonderful plans for you. He daydreams about you. He respects you. That's why you have a free will. He values you. That's why he offered Jesus for you. He loves you. That's why he created you in his image. I hope and pray that you will put your hand in his hand and walk through every day with him.

Alex Beam was a senior in high school when he sketched the illustrations for this book. He is the son of Dr. Ted Beam, the author of this book, and Debbie Beam.

Alex grew up participating in Cub Scouts and Boy Scouts gaining his Eagle Scout rank two weeks before his eighteenth birthday. He enjoyed learning many things with each merit badge and with each rank advancement, including wilderness survival, woodcarving, and SCUBA diving. You can tell that he used the skills gained in his art merit badge to help sketch the illustrations for this book.

Alex is a Kentucky Colonel, the highest honor given to a citizen by the governor of Kentucky. He also has been recognized by the Kentucky House of Representatives for the Outstanding Youth Leadership Award.

Alex has always been involved with his church (he had to because his dad was always the pastor). He enjoyed participating in the children's ministries and youth ministries, helping with skits and holiday plays. For several summers, he attended church camp where he enjoyed white water rafting, water skiing, spelunking, rock climbing, and many games.

Alex enjoyed playing football and basketball, wrestling, and running the hurdles and relays on the track team throughout middle school and high school.

Alex has traveled with mission teams to Oklahoma to work with the Native American Otoe Tribe within the Pawnee Nation and to Peru to work among the people in Lima, Boca Colorado, and Santa Rosa. He has toured the Inca citadel of Machu Picchu and has toured many historic sites in Israel and Egypt. He enjoyed swimming in the Dead Sea, cruising on the Nile River, riding a camel near the Pyramids of Giza, and climbing on the Great Pyramid.

Alex collects knives from all over the world and is presently a student at Lindsey Wilson College in Kentucky where he plans to continue competing in track and field. He wants to manage and run his own business someday.

ABOUT THE AUTHOR

Dr. Ted Beam is married to the smartest girl in his sixth-grade class and his high school sweetheart, Debbie. They also attended their senior prom together. They have four children: Ariel, Alexander, Alissa, and Amelia.

Dr. Beam has earned a bachelor of science degree in industrial technology from Ohio Northern University and was trained to teach kindergarten through twelfth grade. He has earned a master of divinity degree, a master of arts in biblical studies degree, and a doctor of ministry degree, all from Asbury Theological Seminary.

Dr. Beam is an ordained elder in the United Methodist Church, having served in full-time pastoral ministry since 1991. He has volunteered in ministry as a chaplain in local jails and prisons, teaching Bible studies and leading recovery ministries. He has served as a volunteer chaplain for emergency responders. He has guest lectured at Lindsey Wilson College, Campbellsville University, and Asbury Theological Seminary.

Dr. Beam has served on the clergy teams of many Walk to Emmaus weekends and Chrysalis Flight weekends. He has served on many short-term mission teams in Asia, Africa, Central America, and South America, specializing in teaching inductive Bible study techniques to over a thousand pastors.

Dr. Beam has toured the Holy Land three times, drinking water from Jacob's Well, cruising on a fishing boat across the Sea of Galilee, swimming in the Dead Sea, and walking into Jesus's empty tomb. One of those trips was to fulfill a lifelong dream to experience Bethlehem on Christmas Eve. For over an hour on that Christmas Eve, he sat in the room where Jesus was born.